Basic To *Gourmet*

by Richard Erickson

D0189059

AMERICAN
★COOKING★
GUILD™

Boynton Beach, Florida

Acknowledgments
—Cover Design and Layout by Pearl & Associates, Inc.
—Cover Photo by Burwell and Burwell
—Edited by Jeannine Winquist
—Illustrations by Mary Ann Shea Erickson

Revised Edition 1997
Copyright © 1985 by Richard Erickson, rev. 2nd ed. 1993
Printed in U.S.A.
ISBN 0-942320-19-0

More...Quick Recipes for Creative Cooking!
The American Cooking Guild's *Collector's Series* includes over 30 popular cooking topics such as Barbeque, Breakfast & Brunches, Chicken, Cookies, Hors d' Oeuvres, Seafood, Tea, Coffee, Pasta, Pizza, Salads, Italian and many more. Each book contains more than 50 selected recipes. For a catalog of these and many other full sized cookbooks, send $1 to the address below and a coupon will be included for $1 off your first order.

Cookbooks Make Great Premiums!
The American Cooking Guild has been the premier publisher of private label and custom cookbooks since 1981. Retailers, manufacturers, and food companies have all chosen The American Cooking Guild to publish their premium and promotional cookbooks. For further information on our special market programs, please contact the address below.

The American Cooking Guild
3600-K South Congress Avenue
Boynton Beach, FL 33426

Table of Contents

INTRODUCTION

Pizza! Just saying it puts a smile on your face. Delicious, inexpensive and wholesome, pizza is in many ways the perfect food.

And as if that weren't enough, it's fun! Fun to eat and fun to make! Whether you wash it down with cold soda, beer, or a bottle of good wine, pizza fits all tastes and budgets.

The question arises—with all the pizza stands and parlors in America, why go to the trouble of making it yourself? Try it once and find out. You may never eat restaurant pizza again!

The truth is, pizza is easy to make. And just wait until you taste the difference. Freshly baked crusts, rich and flavorful sauces, and the right amount of your favorite topping. From the first time I baked my own pizza, I was hooked.

Pizza means pie in Italian, and like many international foods, it has been so thoroughly absorbed into our culture (and stomachs) that I think it's safe to call it an all-American food by now. Like a pie it has a crust and is topped or filled with delicious ingredients. Long relegated to fast food parlors and stand-up eateries, pizza has surfaced in some of the country's newest and trendiest restaurants as a gourmet entrée.

With this book you will learn the basic techniques of pizza making which will free you to create the ultimate pizza of your own design. Do you like the thin New York-style pizza or a heartier Chicago-style deep-dish pizza? Maybe you'd prefer to make a Tex-Mex style pizza or something in the California nouvelle style? Keep reading and be prepared to make more than one pizza, because when they're home baked the slices go fast.

How To Use This Book

This book is more than just a collection of recipes. Yes, there are many recipes included. In fact, with the different sections on crusts, sauces, and toppings you will be able to produce any kind of pizza imaginable. Think of this as a how-to book. Once you've mastered some simple techniques you will be free to create your own recipes.

The first chapter deals with crusts. The crust is the foundation upon which the pizza is built. Choose the kind of crust you want according to the toppings you want and also according to whether you will serve it as an appetizer or main course. Certain types of crusts naturally go better with certain sauces or toppings, so follow some guidelines at first, then go on to invent your own.

Next come the sauces. Anyone who has ever made a spaghetti sauce can make a pizza sauce, it's easy! And if you think tomato is the only kind of sauce you can make, just wait!

Finally come the toppings. From simple grated mozarella cheese to more elaborately composed toppings, we'll show you how best to do it.

So read through this book at least once to locate the recipes that must appeal to you, then assemble the appropriate ingredients and tools.

BUON APPETITO!!!

Tools & Equipment

I made my first pizza on a cheap aluminum cookie sheet and the results were fine, but good tools really help to make the job easier and the results more consistent. Once you start to make more of your own pizzas you will probably want to invest in better tools.

- A **large, heavy-duty spatula** is indispensable for serving and also for transferring pizzas from cooking to serving platters.

- A good **pizza cutter** will have a sturdy cutting wheel with a sharp blade, but keep in mind that the right knife can do the job just as well. (I prefer to use a bread knife.)

- **Rolling pins** are essential for even crusts. Marble is the best for pastry crusts; any kind will work well for yeast crusts.

- A **cheese grater** with different sized openings, or a **food processor** with a variety of grating attachments.

- A **pastry brush** for brushing olive oil onto the dough.

- I like to use a **large wooden cutting board** as my serving tray. It looks quite attractive and I can cut and serve the pizza right from the board.

- A **large mixing bowl,** either glass or stainless steel, is necessary for mixing the dough and also for letting it rise.

- A **pastry cutter** or **dough scraper** is a small flexible steel strip, usually with a wooden handle. It is perfect for scraping up bits of dough that are stuck to the work surface.

- A **thermometer** is always handy to have in any kitchen, especially if you have trouble guessing just how hot the water for the yeast should be. (One that measures meat and roasts is the right temperature range.)

- A **wooden spoon** for mixing the dough and an assortment of **measuring spoons and cups** for dry and liquid ingredients, and **plastic wrap** to cover the doughs while they are rising.

- A **work surface** for kneading the doughs. The traditional marble or butcher block, stainless steel or formica will all work well.

PIZZA PANS & STONES

Pizza pans should be heavy enough not to warp under the high temperatures necessary for baking pizzas. **Black steel** is generally accepted to be the best because it retains and distributes heat evenly. Black steel pans need extra care to prevent scratches, which turn to rusty spots.

Stainless steel or **aluminum** work almost as well as black steel, but they tend to reflect heat rather than absorb it. Stainless steel and aluminum pans must be well oiled and sprinkled with cornmeal before baking. Remove pizzas from these pans as soon as they come out of the oven to avoid steaming the crusts, which will cause them to be soggy.

Whatever you use for baking, avoid cutting pizza on the pan, because little nicks from cutting will eventually cause crusts to stick to the pan.

For deep-dish pizzas look for black steel pans with 2-inch sides. They are available in various diameters.

Pizza pans need not necessarily be round. Rectangular baking sheets of sufficient thickness are also perfect for pizza, just different.

Another pizza pan I have used with great success is one with holes in the bottom. The holes allow steam to escape, which helps to prevent soggy crusts. These are generally available in supermarkets for heating up frozen pizzas.

Pizza stones are the best way for home bakers to duplicate the conditions of a professional oven. The clays with which the stones are made distribute heat evenly and absorb moisture—important features for achieving crisp crusts. Used in conjunction with a pizza screen, which is an inexpensive wire mesh, the stone can heat in the oven while you are assembling the pizza on the screen. The screen makes it simple to transfer the pizza on and off of the stone, allowing you to make several pizzas while the stone remains in the oven and hot. Screens come in various diameters and are economical enough that I recommend buying several.

Making the Perfect Crust

• The crust is the foundation on which you will build your pizza, so follow the directions carefully the first time through. No two pizza makers produce quite the same crust even though their recipes may be similar, if not identical. The trick is in the quality and handling of the ingredients. The following is a list of guidelines for producing light and crispy crusts the very first time.

• The flour should always be unbleached white flour unless otherwise specified. All-purpose flour is fine for pastry crusts but unbleached flour has a higher gluten content which contributes to crispier yeast crusts.

• To my mind, cake yeast has more flavor but its quality is inconsistent as a result of unreliable handling by suppliers. I prefer to stick with granulated active dry yeast; however, the two are interchangeable, so use whichever you prefer. Just be sure to check the expiration date on whatever you buy. One 2-ounce cake equals three $1/4$-ounce packages of granulated dry yeast.

• Active dry yeast need not be proofed but you should always proof cake yeast. Proofing is a procedure by which you "prove" whether or not the yeast is still effective. Into one cup of warm water (110-115°F) crumble the yeast. Add a pinch of sugar. This gives the yeast, which is a living fungus, carbohydrates to feed on. After about five minutes the yeast should be bubbling and foaming. If it is not, either the yeast is no longer effective or the water temperature was off. Too cold a temperature will not activate the yeast and too hot will kill it.

• Kneading dough is a rhythmic pushing, twisting, and folding action which develops the gluten in the flour. Too much kneading will overdevelop the gluten and make it tough. Usually 10-15 minutes is sufficient.

• To knead, fold the dough over towards you and press with the heel of the hand. Then give it a quarter turn, fold and press again. Continue this procedure rhythmically until the dough becomes smooth and elastic. The dough will seem to have a life of its own, which in fact it does! Add flour as required, but do so sparingly.

• Knead the dough until it is no longer sticky, adding as little flour as possible. If the dough no longer holds together or starts to flake apart, you've added too much flour. Moisten your hands, pat the dough into a ball and leave it to rise.

- The most common cause of a heavy leaden crust is too much flour. A soft, slightly moist dough will make for a lighter chewier crust.

- Yeast gives off tiny bubbles of carbon dioxide, which causes the dough to rise. Lightly oil a bowl that is large enough for the dough to double in bulk.

- Dough should rise in a warm draft-free place. A gas oven with a pilot light is perfect. The bowl should be covered with plastic wrap which helps keep the dough moist and seals in the carbon dioxide.

- Do not let the dough rise to more than double in bulk or it may collapse. Refrigerate the dough if you do not plan to use it immediately or if you wish to prolong the rising. Generally it will take from 45 minutes to $1\frac{1}{2}$ hours for the dough to double in size. You may also punch the dough down and allow it to rise again, for an even lighter crust.

- When rolling out the dough lightly dust it, the work surface, and your rolling pin with flour. Pick the dough up, move it around, flip it over, stretching it out and redusting to keep it from sticking. Allow the dough to relax, or shrink a bit, before transferring it to your baking pan or pizza screen.

- Don't roll or stretch the dough too thin. Less than $\frac{1}{8}$-inch thick and the pizza will leak. If you should tear it or poke a hole in the dough, just pinch it closed.

- Another easy way to shape the dough is to flatten it directly on the pan. Pushing from the center, work the dough into the desired shape. This is particularly effective for deep-dish pizzas. Don't try this on a pizza screen, however, or it will stick in the wire mesh and be impossible to remove.

- If using a baking sheet or aluminum pizza pan, brush liberally with oil and sprinkle lightly with coarsely ground cornmeal, to prevent the pizza from sticking. Pizza stones should be lightly dusted with cornmeal. Pizza screens must be lightly oiled.

Dough can be kneaded in a mixer or food processor, but try it once by hand and experience the difference. Your two hands are the most valuable and sensitive cooking utensils you'll ever possess.

Step 1

Steps 2 & 3

PIZZA CRUSTS

BASIC PIZZA DOUGH

1	cup warm water
1	packet granulated active dry yeast
2¹/₂-3	cups unbleached flour
2	Tablespoons olive oil, plus oil for greasing the bowl and pizza pan
¹/₂	teaspoon salt
	cornmeal for dusting the pizza pan or stone

1. Place the water (about 110-115°) in a 2-quart mixing bowl, and sprinkle the yeast over the top. Mix gently until fully dissolved. Stir in half the flour, 2 tablespoons oil and the salt. Using a wooden spoon combine well, then gradually add the rest of the flour.

2. The dough should now be a large sticky mass and might appear to be a hopeless mess. Don't despair! When it begins to stick together and come away from the sides of the bowl, turn it out on a floured surface and begin to knead.

3. Knead, following all of the instructions on page 8 until the dough is no longer sticky. Place the ball of dough in a 3 quart bowl which has been lightly oiled, rolling the ball around until the surface is coated with oil. Cover the top of the bowl with plastic wrap and let stand in a warm place for about 1¹/₂-2 hours, or until doubled in size.

4. Uncover the bowl and punch down the risen dough, expelling the gases. The dough is now ready to be used. (For a finer textured crust allow the dough to rise a second or even a third time. The subsequent risings will take much less time.)

5. Place the dough on a lightly floured work surface and cut it in half. Starting in the middle and working outwards, roll each half into a circle slightly larger than your baking pan. Allow the dough to "relax" for a minute or two before

transferring it to a pizza pan. If using a pan, oil it and sprinkle lightly with the cornmeal. If using a screen, brush lightly with oil. You are now ready to assemble your pizza.

Yield: two 12-inch pizzas

Variations

Many ingredients can be kneaded into Basic Pizza Dough for some surprisingly delicious variations. Lightly sautéed onions, herbs, black pepper, prosciutto, salami, spinach, and hard cheeses such as Parmesan or Romano. Prepare the dough as normal, allowing it to rise, then punch it down and knead in the ingredient of your choice. Let rise again before rolling it out.

Step 4

Step 5

FOOD PROCESSOR METHOD

Read the manufacturers directions for your food processor to see if it is sturdy enough to handle pizza dough. This procedure works with any of the crusts and is quicker than the time it takes to assemble all the ingredients.

1. Using a steel blade or special dough blade, pour warm water and the yeast into the bowl and pulse a couple of times until the yeast is dissolved.

2. Add all but 3 tablespoons of the flour, plus the oil and the salt, then process until the dough forms a ball or a layer around the blade. Test the dough with your finger to see if it is sticky and if so add the rest of the flour. If it is too dry, add a tablespoon of water at a time until a smooth elastic quality is achieved.

3. Turn the dough out of the bowl, and with lightly floured hands knead it into a ball shape. Place in an oiled bowl, cover and let rest. Proceed with the Basic Pizza Dough recipe from step 4.

Yield: two 12-inch pizzas

WHOLE WHEAT PIZZA DOUGH

Here is a crust for those who prefer whole wheat. Never use only whole wheat flour as the flavor overwhelms the other ingredients and it does not produce a good crust. For variety, try substituting rye, soy, rice or any other flour for the whole wheat in this recipe.

1	*cup warm water*
1	*packet active dry yeast*
1	*cup whole wheat bread flour*
1$^1/_2$	*cups (approximately) unbleached flour*
$^1/_2$	*teaspoon salt*
2	*Tablespoons olive oil*

Sift together the flours and the salt, then follow the directions in the Basic Pizza Dough recipe on page 10.

Yield: two 12-inch pizzas

SPINACH CRUST

Here is a crust to make your pizzas uniquely yours. It requires no rising time, and it can be made in less time than it takes to defrost the spinach.

1	*package (10 ounces) frozen, thawed chopped spinach*
$^1/_4$	*cup butter*
$^1/_2$	*cup milk*
1	*large egg*
2	*cups all-purpose flour*
3	*teaspoons baking powder*
$^1/_2$	*teaspoon salt*

1. Preheat overn to 450°.

2. Drain spinach in a colander and squeeze in paper towels or with hands to remove all moisture.

3. In a small pan melt butter, stir in spinach and cook over low heat for 5 minutes. Remove from heat and stir in milk and egg.

4. In a large bowl combine 1$^3/_4$ cups of the flour with the baking powder and salt, mix well and add the spinach mixture. Reserve $^1/_4$ cup of the flour to make a firmer dough, if needed.

5. Grease a 12-inch pizza pan or a 10 x 14-inch cookie sheet. Place dough on pan and cover with wax paper. Roll out to an even layer pushing up around the edges to form a border. Remove the wax paper.

6. Bake crust in a preheated 450° oven for approximately 15-20 minutes, then add toppings and bake until done.

Yield: one 12-inch pizza

Basic Pastry Crust

Although more commonly used for desserts and pastry, this crust is also marvelous as a pizza crust. It works especially well for mini pizzas as hors d'oeuvres. Being a non-yeast crust, it is easier to handle and takes only minutes to prepare.

>   3   cups all-purpose flour
> $1/2$ teaspoon salt
> $1/2$ cup unsalted butter, chilled
>   8   Tablespoons ice water
>   2   egg yolks

1. Preheat oven to 375°.

2. Combine the flour and salt in the container of a food processor. Cut the butter into small pieces and add, processing in short bursts. Continuing the pulse motion, add the egg yolks and ice water, blending just until pastry pulls away from the sides of the bowl.

3. If a food processor is not used, place flour, salt and butter in a mixing bowl. Cut the butter in with a pastry blender until it has the texture of coarse oatmeal. Rapidly beat in the egg yolks and water with a fork.

4. Gather the dough together in a flat round, wrap in wax paper, and chill for at least one hour before using. (This dough freezes beautifully, so make a double batch and have some on hand for later use.)

5. Roll out the dough or press it into a tart pan, to a thickness of $1/8$-inch. Fill and bake.

Yield: two 8- or 9-inch tarts

Having trouble with soggy crusts? Try putting the cheese on first, then the sauces and toppings. This helps ensure a crispy crust by sealing out the liquids.

CREAM CHEESE CRUST

Use this crust just as you would the Basic Pastry Crust. Try using a garlic or herbed cream cheese for an unusual variation.

$3/4$ *cup unsalted butter*
3   *ounces cream cheese*
2   *cups all-purpose flour*

1. Preheat oven to 375°.

2. Cut the butter and cream cheese into small pieces. Combine everything in a large mixing bowl. With a pastry cutter blend until the dough achieves the consistency of oatmeal. Wrap in wax paper and chill for at least one hour before using.

3. Roll out the dough or press it into a tart pan to a $1/8$-inch thickness. Fill and bake.

Yield: two 8- or 9-inch tarts

ZUCCHINI CRUST

1   *package active dry yeast*
1   *cup warm water*
2   *medium zucchinis, grated*
     salt
2   *Tablespoons olive oil*
$2^1/2$ *cups (approximately) unbleached flour*

1. Dissolve the yeast in the cup of warm water.

2. Mix grated zucchini with a liberal amount of salt and let stand in a colander for at least 15 minutes. Rinse and squeeze dry using paper towels.

3. Mix the grated zucchini with the olive oil, add the yeast mixture, and 2 cups of the flour. Turn the dough out on a floured work surface and begin kneading. Continue adding more flour a little at a time until the dough no longer sticks.

4. Place the dough in a 3-quart oiled bowl, cover with plastic wrap, and let rise until doubled in size, about $1^1/2$-2 hours.

5. Punch down and use as you would a basic pizza crust.

Yield: two 12-inch pizzas

Cornmeal Crust

This crust is well suited to Tex-Mex style toppings. It also works very well in deep-dish style pizzas. In Italy this is called polenta and is usually made with milk and water then flavored with Parmesan. Either way it is delicious and delightfully different.

> 2   *cups water, or 1 cup water and 1 cup milk*
> $^1/_2$ *teaspoon salt*
> 1   *cup yellow cornmeal*
>   *optional: $^1/_4$ cup parmesan with 1 whole egg, beaten*

1. Preheat the oven to 400°. Prepare the pan by lightly oiling it and sprinkling with cornmeal.

2. Bring the water and/or milk and the salt to a boil. Gradually pour in the cornmeal, remove from heat and mix with a wire wisk until a smooth, stiff dough is formed. If using the parmesan and egg, add at this point.

3. Place mixture in the pizza pan, oil your hands, and press the cornmeal dough into the pan forming an edge by pressing up the sides.

4. Bake for about 20-25 minutes.

5. Now add your toppings or deep-dish fillings and bake for another 20-30 minutes.

Yield: two 8-inch or one 12-inch pizza

TORTE CRUST

This crust makes a heavenly Torte Rustica. It can also be used for quiches.

> 2   *cups unbleached white flour*
> 2   *Tablespoons all-purpose flour*
> 2   *teaspoons baking powder*
> $^1/_2$ *cup (1 stick) butter, chilled*
> 2   *eggs, beaten*
> 1   *egg yolk*

1. Sift together the dry ingredients.

2. Cut the butter into bits and combine with dry ingredients, using a pastry blender, until the mixture is the consistency of coarse oatmeal.

3. Add the eggs and egg yolk, mixing until everything holds together.

4. Wrap in wax paper and chill for 30 minutes. Then press into a pie pan, reserving about half to roll out for the top if making a double crusted pie.

5. Fill and bake at 400°.

Yield: one 8- to 10-inch double-crusted pie

Egg Crust

This is a rich and delicious crust, made with whole eggs, that is similar to a brioche in texture. It is particularly suited to deep-dish or double-crusted pizzas like the Torte Rustica, or the French Pissaladiere.

$4^1/_2$ cups flour
    1   Tablespoon sugar
        pinch of salt
$^1/_2$ cup (1 stick) butter, softened
$1^1/_2$ packages active dry yeast
$^1/_4$ cup milk, warmed to 110°
    4   large whole eggs

1. In a large bowl combine the flour, the sugar, and a pinch salt. Add the softened butter and beat until it resembles coarse meal.

2. Mix the yeast in the milk and let dissolve.

3. Beat the eggs and add to the flour mixture. Now add the yeast and combine to form a very stiff dough.

4. Turn out on a lightly floured work surface and knead for at least 10 minutes. Then put in a well oiled bowl, cover, and leave to rise until doubled in size. Punch down and use as you would Basic Pizza Dough. Do not bake over 400° or it will burn.

Yield: two thick-crusted 12-inch pizzas

SOURDOUGH CRUST

For an extraordinary combination, serve this crust with Sauce Putanesca, page 22.

    1   cup Sourdough Starter (recipe follows)
    3/4 cup warm water
    3   cups unbleached white flour, plus flour
        for kneading
    1/2 teaspoon salt
    2   Tablespoons oil or lard

1. Combine the sourdough starter with $1/2$ cup of the water and 1 cup of the flour. Stir to blend and cover with plastic wrap for about 2 hours.

2. Add the salt, oil, remaining flour and water and blend well. Turn the mixture out onto a lightly floured board and knead for 10 to 15 minutes, adding flour as necessary.

3. Shape the mixture into a ball, put into an oiled bowl and let rise, covered, until it has doubled in bulk, about $1 1/2$ hours. Punch the dough down and use as for Basic Pizza Dough.

Yield: two 12-inch pizzas

Sourdough Starter

    1   package active dry yeast
    2   cups water, warmed to 110-115°
    2   cups flour, preferably whole wheat, rye or
        a mixture
    1   Tablespoon sugar or honey

1. Dissolve the yeast in $1/2$ cup water. Stir in the remaining $1 1/2$ cups of water, the flour and sugar or honey. Beat until smooth and well-blended.

2. Cover with plastic wrap and let stand at room temperature for about 48 hours. Stir the mixture 2 or 3 times each day.

When properly fermented and "sour" it will be bubbly on top. This might take up to a week, depending on humidity, room temperature, etc. Store the starter in the refrigerator, covered with cheesecloth or a loose plastic wrap. When part of the starter is removed, add 1 cup flour and 1 cup water, stirring

to incorporate and let stand at room temperature until the fermentation is resumed. The starter may be used and replenished indefinitely, and it improves with age.

CHICAGO STYLE DEEP-DISH CRUST

The addition of cornmeal and oil give this crust its rich biscuit-like qualities. This dough is always pressed into the pan and allowed to rest 5-10 minutes before baking.

   1   package active dry yeast
   1   cup water, warmed to 110-115°
   2¹/₂   cups flour
   ¹/₂   cup yellow cornmeal
   1   teaspoon salt
   4   Tablespoons olive oil

1. Mix the yeast and water and let dissolve.

2. Combine all ingredients in a large mixing bowl, adding the flour a little at a time. Mix well until the dough comes away from the sides of the bowl.

3. Turn out onto a lightly floured work surface and knead the dough until it is no longer sticky, about 10-15 minutes.

4. Put the dough in an oiled bowl, turning to coat well with oil, cover with plastic wrap and let rise.

5. When the dough has doubled in size punch it down and, with lightly oiled hands, press the dough into and up the sides of the deep-dish pans.

6. Preheat the oven to 475°.

7. Let the dough relax for 10 minutes or so (it will actually start to rise a bit again), fill with the ingredients of your choice and bake for 15 minutes at 475°. Then lower the oven to 400° and let bake for another 20-25 minutes.

Yield: two 10-inch deep-dish pizza pans

Sauces

When I first started making pizzas I used to drown them in sauce, a natural reaction to never having enough on pizzeria pizzas. I've calmed down a bit now, although I do like a heartier, zestier sauce than most people. There are many sauces that can be used with pizza but the thing to remember is balance. Balance the flavors so that subtle tastes do not become lost. If you like pizza covered with mushrooms, for example, stick to a milder sauce that won't overwhelm the delicacy of the mushrooms.

Sauces for pizza should be fairly thick, as thin soupy sauces soak right into the crust, making it soggy. There are two ways to thicken sauces: the first is to cook the sauce down, reducing the amount of liquid by evaporation. The second is to use a thickening agent, such as tomato paste, to bring the sauce to the proper consistency.

One word of caution: always use stainless steel saucepans when cooking with tomatoes as the acid in tomatoes reacts with aluminum and causes a bitter taste. Tomato sauces also tend to splatter so be sure to keep the heat low. One of these days I'll get around to buying a splatter screen,which would seem to be the best solution. Pizza sauces lend themselves particularly well to being made in large batches, which can then be put into smaller containers and refrigerated or frozen. Sauces keep well, although they do lose a bit of flavor after defrosting, so check the seasonings and correct if necessary.

Purists may scream, but in my estimation a pizza sauce is not that much different from a spaghetti sauce, just a bit thicker perhaps. That being the case, consider using a leftover spaghetti sauce for pizza or vice versa.

Lastly, please do not think that every pizza must have a sauce. Try topping one with chunks of fresh or canned tomatoes, or cheese and a bit of olive oil for a "pizza bianco."

A good quality olive oil is essential in the preparation of pizza. Virgin or extra-virgin oils are excellent in doughs but not for sautéing, because they have a low burning point. For sautéing I use a good "pure" olive oil, which has a higher burning point, and a nice light olive flavor. Any Italian olive oil from Lucca will be good, such as Bertolli or Berio.

Basic Pizza Sauce

A well seasoned sauce is the key to great pizza. This sauce is simple to prepare, quick to cook, and versatile enough to be used with almost any pizza you make. (Try doubling this recipe, because it freezes well.)

> 1   *medium onion, finely chopped*
> 2   *Tablespoons olive oil*
> 1   *28-ounce can Italian-style tomatoes, packed in purée (if packed in juice, add 2 Tablespoons tomato paste.)*
> 1   *clove garlic, minced*
> 1   *teaspoon dried oregano or marjoram*
> 1   *teaspoon dried basil*
> 1   *bay leaf*
>   *freshly ground pepper, to taste*

1. In a 2 or 3-quart stainless steel saucepan, lightly sauté the onions in the olive oil over medium heat until translucent.
2. Coarsely chop the tomatoes, then add the tomatoes and purée to the sautéed onions. Add the garlic and seasonings and bring to a simmer.
3. Stir occasionally to prevent the sauce from sticking to the bottom of the pan and burning.
4. Lower the heat and simmer the sauce uncovered, for about 20-30 minutes.

Yield: approximately 3 cups of sauce

Variation: For a spicier sauce add red pepper flakes or cayenne to taste.

SAUCE PUTANESCA

A wonderful southern Italian favorite. Don't be put off by the anchovies, even if you're not an anchovy lover. The flavors melt together to create an incredibly delicious sauce that is easy to make.

Directions: Proceed as with the Basic Pizza Sauce recipe (page 21) through step #2. Add one small tin anchovies, finely chopped; 2 tablespoons capers, and about 15 oil-cured black olives, pitted. Add a dash of red wine and let simmer for about 30 minutes or until the flavors are married.

VEGETABLE PIZZA SAUCE

This is a wonderfully flavorful sauce. Try it on linguini as well.

4	Tablespoons olive oil
1	medium onion, finely chopped
$1/2$	cup finely chopped celery
$1/2$	cup grated carrot
$1/2$	cup finely chopped red or green pepper
$1/2$	cup finely grated zucchini
1	clove garlic, finely chopped
1	teaspoon oregano
	salt and freshly ground pepper, to taste
1	28-ounce can plum tomatoes in puree

1. Heat the oil in a medium sauce pan. Over medium heat add the onions and celery. Sauté until translucent.

2. Add the rest of the vegetables and continue cooking until limp but not brown.

3. Add the garlic, seasonings, and tomatoes. Simmer over low heat for about 20-30 minutes. (When in season, add $1/4$ cup chopped fresh basil.)

Yield: approximately 4 cups sauce

Sun-Dried Tomato Sauce

This sauce is sublime! In fact, it is so flavorful that there is no need to add salt, pepper, or spices. Just allow the rich taste of the sundried tomatoes to come through. This is also good with pasta and seems to combine particularly well with sausage and goat cheese.

> 1   cup sun-dried tomatoes packed in oil, drained
>
> 1   cup water
>
> 1   cup tomato sauce

1. Cook the sun-dried tomatoes in 1 cup water, uncovered, for about 20 minutes, or until plump and tender.

2. Reduce the heat, add the tomato sauce and let simmer for another 10 minutes.

3. Pour the contents into the container of a food processor or blender and process.

Yield: about 2 cups

MORNAY SAUCE

This is a white cheese sauce that is normally made with egg yolks. I leave them out, because eggs tend to curdle or harden under the high heat needed to bake pizza. I recommend this sauce for deep dish pizzas, calzone (page 60) and panzerotti (page 63).

  2   Tablespoons unsalted butter
  2   Tablespoons all-purpose flour
  1   cup milk
  $^1/_2$ cup heavy cream
  $^1/_4$ cup grated gruyere or cheddar cheese
       salt, pepper, and a pinch of cayenne

1. Melt the butter in a small saucepan and add the flour, whisking until well blended.
2. Add the milk slowly, continuing to whisk rapidly.
3. When thickened, add the cream continuing to whisk. Remove from the heat and incorporate the cheese and spices.

Yield: about 2 cups

SPINACH SAUCE

This is one of my favorite sauces with which to make deep-dish pizzas or calzone (page 60). Be prepared to pass the recipe on, because everyone wants to know how it is made. Spinach Sauce also goes well with pastas like fusilli or shells.

  2   Tablespoons unsalted butter
  2   Tablespoons flour
  1   cup milk
  1   10-ounce package frozen chopped
       spinach, defrosted and drained
  $^1/_4$ cup heavy cream
  $^1/_4$ cup grated parmesan
       salt, pepper, and a pinch of nutmeg

1. Melt the butter over low heat in a medium saucepan, add the flour and whisk until thoroughly blended.

2. Add the milk slowly, continuing to whisk until smooth.

3. When thickened, add the spinach and the cream. Simmer for about five minutes then add the cheese and spices to taste.

Yield: about 2¹/₂ cups

CREOLE SAUCE

This is another versatile sauce that is equally at home on pasta or rice. Use it to top the Deep-Dish Crust (page 19) or Cornmeal Crust (page 16). Add shrimp for a for a real treat.

3   Tablespoons olive oil
¹/₂   cup finely chopped onion
¹/₂   cup finely chopped celery
¹/₂   cup diced green or red pepper
¹/₄   teaspoon thyme
¹/₄   teaspoon basil
1   bay leaf
      salt and freshly ground pepper, to taste
¹/₂   teaspoon cayenne
1   14-ounce can whole tomatoes
3   ounces tomato paste
      grated rind and juice from half a lemon
      hot sauce, to taste
2   Tablespoons finely chopped parsley

1. Heat the olive oil in a medium saucepan and sauté the onions, celery, and red or green pepper over medium heat until soft. Crumble in the spices, stirring for another minute.

2. Add the tomatoes, tomato paste, lemon juice and rind, cover and simmer on low for about 30 minutes.

3. After 30 minutes, check the seasoning and add the hot sauce, to taste. Stir in the fresh parsley.

Yield: approximately 3¹/₄ cups sauce

ENCHILADA SAUCE

$1/3$ cup powdered red chili
1   Tablespoon all-purpose flour
$3/4$ cup water
2   Tablespoons bacon fat or lard
$1/2$ cup finely minced onion
1   clove garlic, minced
$1/2$ teaspoon oregano
      salt, to taste

1. Mix the chili powder and flour with enough water to make a thin sauce. (You can substitute one cup of fresh chili paste for the chili powder, flour and water mixture.

2. In a small saucepan, heat the bacon fat and sauté the onion until translucent.

3. Now add the garlic, oregano, salt and the chili sauce or paste. Simmer uncovered for about 30 minutes or until the sauce has thickened.

Yield: about 1 cup

PESTO

Pesto is something no kitchen should be without. Pesto freezes beautifully, so it is a good idea to make large batches when fresh basil is in season. I fill dozens of small and medium size plastic containers to pull out of the freezer as I need them. Pesto is excellent served on pasta, and works best with deep-dish pizzas or calzone as it tends to dry out on thin crusted pizzas.

2	cups fresh basil
$1/2$	cup fresh parsley
$1/4$	cup pine nuts or walnuts
2	cloves garlic
$3/4$	cup fresh parmesan cheese, grated
$1/2$	cup olive oil
3	Tablespoons unsalted butter, softened
	salt, to taste

Remove all the tough stems from the basil and pack the leaves into a 2-cup measuring cup. Combine basil with all remaining ingredients in the bowl of a food processor and blend on high speed until evenly combined.

Yield: approximately 2$1/2$ cups

There is no substitute for fresh garlic. Do yourself a favor and get rid of garlic powder or garlic salt. They have an unpleasant, disagreeable taste and certainly contribute nothing to home-made pizza.

TOPPINGS

Here's where the real fun begins! There is no limit to what you can put on your pizza, although there are certain tried and true combinations that always work well together. Most importantly, use quality ingredients, and take care handling them. Following are some guidelines that should help you get started.

CHEESES

Try putting soft cheeses in the freezer for about 20-30 minutes and they will be much easier to grate.

Mozzarella is the most popular cheese for pizza, and with good reason. It melts well, and its subtle flavor blends deliciously with the crust, tomato sauce and almost any ingredient you can imagine. Avoid skim-milk mozzarella, as it tends to become hard and stringy after melting. For a special treat try freshly made mozarella, smoked or buffalo-milk mozzarella.

Parmesan should be well aged, and always freshly grated, never out of a box or can. Parmesan and other hard cheeses, like **Romano,** need to be combined with a softer cheese that melts well or, if used alone, grated on just a few minutes before removing the pizza from the oven.

Asiago and **Fontina** are wonderful cheeses, either by themselves or combined with mozzarella.

Provolone is another cheese that melts well and can be used by itself or mixed with mozzarella.

Goat cheese and **blue cheese** are delicious, if non-traditional, cheeses for pizza. Crumble them on by hand.

Ricotta is great with deep-dish pizzas or in fillings for calzone.

Cottage cheese is too salty and too moist for pizza.

Cheddar cheese melts well and combines well with certain American-style ingredients.

Monterey Jack is another delicious melting cheese that has a natural affinity with Mexican-style pizzas.

As you can see, the possibilities are endless, so have fun and explore all options.

VEGETABLES

As with cheeses, I encourage creative experimentation. There are, however, a few rules for using vegetables which are worth knowing. I find that with vegetables such as **onions, zucchini, eggplant,** and **peppers** it is best if they are lightly sautéed before adding them to the pizza. The slight precooking and light coating of oil prevents them from drying out in the oven. Or, lightly steam the vegetables but be careful to remove excess moisture by draining well. Again, a light coating of oil, sauce or cheese helps prevent them from drying out.

FISH

Fresh fish and **shellfish** tend to dry out very quickly at high temperatures. The best solution is to toss them in oil and add them in the last 5-10 minutes of baking. The best **canned fish** for pizza (tuna, sardines, clams, etc.) is packed in oil. If packed in brine, drain then mix in your sauce or coat in oil first.

MEAT

Chicken, beef, pork, sausage, bacon, salami, pepperoni, prosciutto, and even **turkey** are all delicious when added to pizza. Any meat should be cooked first, then added. Meats, like pepperoni, can dry out and even burn so I like to push them down in the sauce a little bit or cover them with cheese first.

NUTS

Sound strange? Try some and see for yourself. Anything could work, but I find that **pumpkin, sesame, sunflower,** and **pine nuts** are the best. Buy them raw. The toasting they get in the oven really brings out their flavor. Or toast them first and sprinkle over a pizza with zucchini for a truly elegant touch.

PUTTING IT ALL TOGETHER

PIZZA NAPOLETANA

We start with the pizza most familiar to all of us. And, like most recipes, there are numerous versions, but the constants remain—crushed tomatoes or tomato sauce and mozzarella cheese. This is a thin crusted pizza that bakes very quickly if your oven is properly heated, so keep an eye on it.

    1   recipe Basic Pizza Dough (page 10)
    1   recipe Basic Pizza Sauce (page 21)
        olive oil
    1   2-ounce can anchovy filets, optional
    1   pound mozzarella, grated

1. Preheat the oven to 450°.

2. Prepare and roll out the pizza dough, brushing the dough lightly with olive oil. If using a pan, brush lightly with oil and sprinkle with cornmeal. If using a screen, brush lightly with oil.

3. Ladle the sauce over the dough, spreading it out as evenly as possible.

4. If using the anchovy filets arrange evenly over the sauce. Then sprinkle the cheese generously to cover the entire surface.

5. Bake for approximately 20 minutes or until the crust is crisp and golden, and the cheese melted. Serve immediately.

Yield: two 12-inch pizzas

PIZZA WITH MUSHROOMS

Use canned only if you must, because fresh mushrooms are what makes this pizza special. Try wild porcini or shitake mushrooms for an extraordinary alternative.

- 1 recipe Basic Pizza Dough (page 10)
- 1 pound fresh mushrooms
- 1 recipe Basic Pizza Sauce (page 21)
- 1 pound mozzarella, grated
- 2 Tablespoons olive oil, plus oil for brushing the pan and dough

1. Preheat the oven to 450°.

2. Prepare the dough and brush lightly with oil.

3. Slice the mushrooms thinly and sauté very lightly in oil. (You may also just toss them with oil in a bowl to lightly coat.)

4. Sauce the pizza and cover with the grated cheese.

5. Toss the mushrooms over the pizza, or if you like, arrange the sliced mushrooms in a pattern to a visually stunning presentation.

6. Bake for about 20 minutes or until done.

Yield: two 12-inch pizzas

Pepperoni Pizza

Pepperoni, one of the most popular pizza toppings, is a smoked sausage with a distinctly spicy flavor. Pepperoni burns quickly on top of pizza, so I add it in the final few minutes of baking to retain its appetizing appearance. An alternate method is to cover with sauce and cheese to maintain moisture.

1   *recipe Basic Pizza Dough (page 10)*
    olive oil
1   *recipe Basic Pizza Sauce (page 21)*
1   *pound mozzarella, grated*
$^1/_4$ *cup parmesan, freshly grated*
1   *pound pepperoni, thinly sliced*

1. Preheat the oven to 450°. Prepare the dough and brush lightly with olive oil.

2. Sauce the pizza, then cover with the grated cheeses.

3. Bake the pizza for 15 minutes, remove and cover with the pepperoni. Return to the oven for about 5 minutes.

Yield: two 12-inch pizzas

Sausage & Pepper Pizza

Another popular pizza, served in pizza shops from coast to coast, that is even better when you make it yourself. This recipe uses fresh instead of dried or smoked sausage. Green bell peppers are fine, but try using red or even yellow for a colorful and festive pizza.

1   recipe Basic Pizza dough (page 10) or
    Whole Wheat Pizza Dough (page 12)
    olive oil
1   pound hot or sweet Italian sausage
1   recipe Basic Pizza Sauce (page 21)
1   pound mozzarella, grated or sliced
2   medium red and or green bell peppers

1. Preheat the oven to 450°. Prepare the dough and brush lightly with olive oil.

2. Extract the sausages from their casings, crumble, and sauté in a lightly oiled skillet until cooked, but not browned. Remove with a slotted spoon to a saucepot and add the sauce. Let simmer for about 15 minutes.

3. Cover pizza with the sauce and top with the grated cheese. Now arrange the peppers over the cheese in a circular pattern. (Or, spell Happy Birthday with the peppers, if that's appropriate. I did one last year with red and green peppers in the shape of a Christmas tree, which was a big hit.)

4. Bake the pizza for about 20 minutes, or until the crust is golden brown and the cheese and sauce are bubbling.

Yield: 2 12-inch pizzas

▟▛▟▛▟▛▟▛▟▛▟▛▟▛▟▛▟▛▟▛

Bacon & Cheddar Pizza

Not very Italian, but that doesn't mean it's not delicious. America's answer to sausage and mozzarella! This pizza is also delicious for breakfast. It could be made with Basic Pizza Dough or a Pastry Crust but is particularly satisfying when paired with the Egg Crust.

    1   recipe Egg Crust (page 17)
        olive oil
    1   pound bacon
    1   large yellow onion, finely diced
    1   pound cheddar cheese, grated
        freshly ground black pepper, to taste

1. Preheat oven to 450°. Prepare the dough and brush lightly with olive oil.

2. Cut the bacon into fourths and very gently cook in a skillet over a low flame until the fat is rendered the the bacon is still soft. Remove with a slotted spoon and drain.

3. Add the onion to the skillet with the bacon fat, and sauté until translucent.

4. Cover the dough with the onions and the bacon pieces. Sprinkle the grated cheese over the top and bake for about 20 minutes. Top with freshly grated black pepper. (For a delicious variation, top with slices of fresh tomato.)

Yield: two 12-inch pizzas

Pizza With Mussels

The White Clam Pizza can be made with fresh or canned clams but this pizza absolutely requires fresh mussels. It works equally well as a deep-dish pizza.

1	recipe Basic Pizza Dough (page 10) or Deep-Dish Style Crust (page 19)
	olive oil
2	cups mussels, cleaned and drained
$1/4$	cup dry white wine
2	Tablespoons garlic, minced
	salt and pepper, to taste
1	recipe Putanesca Sauce (page 22)
$1/2$	cup parmesan, grated

1. Preheat the oven to 450°. Prepare the dough and brush lightly with olive oil.

2. Wash and scrub the mussels, removing their beards. Put them in a large kettle with the white wine, garlic, and a little salt and pepper.

3. Cover and cook over high heat, stirring once or twice, for about five minutes, or until the shells open.

4. Remove the mussels from their shells, reserving the cooking liquid. Strain the cooking liquid through a double layer of cheesecloth.

5. Add this liquid to the Putanesca Sauce and cook for about 15 minutes at a gentle simmer until the sauce has returned to its original consistency.

6. Cover the prepared dough with half of the sauce and bake for about 10 minutes. Remove the pizza from the oven, top with the mussels and the remaining sauce. Sprinkle the Parmesan over all and return to the oven for another 10 minutes.

Yield: two 12-inch pizzas

White Clam Pizza

1	recipe Basic Pizza Dough (page 10)
	olive oil for brushing dough
2	cups chopped fresh clams, or 2 10-ounce cans, drained
2	Tablespoons garlic, minced
4	Tablespoons olive oil
1	teaspoon oregano
	salt and pepper, to taste
12	ounces mozzarella, grated
$^1/_2$	cup parmesan, grated

1. Preheat the oven to 450°. Prepare the dough and brush lightly with olive oil.

2. Combine the clams, garlic, 4 tablespoons olive oil and seasonings in a bowl. Toss well to coat.

3. Cover the dough with the clam mixture and top with the cheeses. Bake for about 15-20 minutes or until the crust is golden and cheese is bubbling.

Yield: two 12-inch pizzas

Quatttro Stagioni

Quattro Stagioni means "Four Seasons." Traditionally, this pizza is divided into four quarters, each with a different topping representing the different seasons. It is a beautiful pizza, perfect for parties, especially if only one of your group is an anchovy lover. It can be made with or without sauce, and the toppings can be adjusted to suit individual tastes.

1	recipe Basic Pizza Dough (page 10) olive oil
1	recipe Basic Pizza Sauce (page 21), optional
1	pound mozzarella, grated
20	black olives
2	ounces anchovy filets
$^1/_2$	pound mushrooms, thickly sliced and lightly sautéed
4	ounces prosciutto, thickly sliced
1	red or green pepper, cut into strips

1. Preheat the oven to 450°. Prepare the dough and brush lightly with olive oil.

2. If using sauce, cover the prepared dough with the sauce, then with the cheese. If not, simply cover with the cheese.

3. Visually divide the pie into quarters and cover each quarter with a different topping.

4. Bake for about 20 minutes or until the crust is golden.

Yield: two 12-inch pizzas

Amalfi Style Pizza

This simple but delicious pizza is made with sardines. Canned sardines are available everywhere and they work just fine, but for a very special treat, if you have a good fish market nearby, try fresh sardines.

> 1 recipe Basic Pizza dough (page 10) or Sourdough Crust (page 18)
> olive oil
> 2 4-ounce tins sardines, packed in oil
> 2 Tablespoons fresh garlic, minced
> 1 pound mozzarella, grated

1. Preheat the oven to 450°. Prepare the dough and brush lightly with olive oil.

2. Toss the sardines and garlic in a bowl. (If using fresh sardines, add 4 tablespoons olive oil and stir to coat the fish.)

3. Cover the prepared dough with the grated cheese and bake for about 10 minutes. Remove from the oven and top with the sardines, return to the oven for another 10 minutes, or until done.

Yield: two 12-inch pizzas

Variation: Cover the prepared dough with Putanesca Sauce (page 22), cover with sardines, and top with the mozzarella.

Eggplant Pizza

> 1 large eggplant, sliced $1/4$-inch thick
> salt
> 1 recipe Whole Wheat Pizza Dough (page 12)
> olive oil for lightly brushing dough
> $1/4$ cup olive oil
> 1 pound mozzarella, grated
> 1 recipe Basic Pizza Sauce (page 21)
> $1/2$ cup parmesan, grated

1. Liberally salt the sliced eggplant and place in a colander to drain excess moisture for at least 20 minutes.

2. Preheat the oven to 450°. Prepare the dough and brush lightly with olive oil. Now rinse the eggplant and pat dry.

3. Heat the oil in a skillet over medium-high heat and sauté the eggplant for about 2-3 minutes on each side.

4. First cover the dough with the mozzarella. Next layer the eggplant slices around the pizza and spoon the sauce over all. Top with the parmesan and bake for about 20 minutes.

Yield: two 12-inch pizzas

SWISS PIZZA

I don't know if you'll ever find this served in Switzerland, but who cares? Swiss cheese is the star in this pizza, so buy the best.

  1   recipe Basic Pizza Dough (page 10) or Egg Crust (page 17)
      olive oil
  1   medium onion, finely chopped
  2   Tablespoons butter
  5   pinches cayenne
  1   pound cooked ham, diced
$^1/_2$ pound gruyere cheese, grated
$^1/_2$ pound emmenthal cheese, grated
      freshly ground black pepper, to taste

1. Preheat the oven to 450°. Prepare the dough and brush lightly with olive oil.

2. In a small sauté pan lightly cook the onion in the butter until translucent. Add the cayenne and ham and stir to combine.

3. Cover the prepared dough with the onion-ham mixture and top with the grated cheeses.

4. Bake for about 20 minutes or until golden. Top with freshly grated black pepper and serve.

Yield: two 12-inch pizzas

Pizza Putanesca

This pizza is particularly well-suited to a sourdough crust. Be prepared to make seconds. This one goes fast!

　1　recipe Sourdough Crust (page 18)
　　　olive oil
　1　pound mozzarella, grated or sliced
　1　recipe Sauce Putanesca (page 22)
　$^1/_2$　cup romano, grated
　$^1/_2$　cup parmesan, grated

1. Preheat the oven to 450°. Prepare the dough and brush lightly with olive oil.

2. Cover the prepared dough with the mozzarella. Spoon the sauce over the cheese, and top with the romano and parmesan.

3. Bake for about 20 minutes or until done.

Yield: two 12-inch pizzas

Pizza Bianca

Pizza bianca means "white pizza." This is as simple as pizza can possibly be. It is made only with the dough, brushed with a bit of olive oil, and seasoned with garlic or some freshly grated cheeses. Romans like their pizzas without tomato sauce. Try it and you'll see why.

I often make little mini Pizza Biancas from leftover pieces of dough, to whet the appetite while we prepare the main course. This is where a good home-made, hand-kneaded crust really shines, as there are no sauces to cover it up.

Gorgonzola Pizza

Gorgonzola is in the blue cheese family. An Italian after dinner cheese, it is similar to Roquefort and Stilton.

- 1 recipe Egg Dough (page 17)
   olive oil
- 1 pound gorgonzola

1. Preheat the oven to 450°. Prepare the dough and brush with olive oil.

2. Bake the pizza for about 5 minutes and remove from the oven. Crumble the cheese over the top and return to the oven for another 10 minutes or until the crust is golden and the cheese melted.

Yield: two 12-inch pizzas

Variation: Substitute brie cheese for the gorgonzola or mix the two cheeses.

Late Night Supper Menu

Gorgonzola Pizza

Arugula Boston lettuce salad

Calif. Zinfandel or Italian Spanna

Fresh fruit

*To peel toma-
toes, dip them
in boiling water
for one minute,
then immediate-
ly plunge them
into ice water.
The skin will
now peel off
easily.*

Pizza With Fresh Tomatoes & Basil

Make this pizza in July and August, when tomatoes
are at their peak and fresh basil its most fragrant.
Use freshly made mozzarella, with its delicate texture and flavor, for the difference between good
pizza and great pizza.

1	recipe Basic Pizza Dough (page 10) olive oil
1	pound mozzarella, sliced or grated
4-5	medium tomatoes, peeled and coarsely chopped
2	Tablespoons garlic, minced
4	Tablespoons fresh basil, coarsely chopped salt and freshly ground pepper, to taste
4	Tablespoons olive oil

1. Preheat the oven to 450°. Prepare the dough and
   brush lightly with olive oil.

2. Cover the pizza with the mozzarella. Now toss all
   the remaining ingredients together in a bowl with
   the 4 tablespoons olive oil.

3. Top the pizza with this mixture and bake for
   about 15-20 minutes or until done.

Yield: two 12-inch pizzas

Sun-Dried Tomato & Goat Cheese Pizza

Sounds simple and it is. The wonderful flavors of
the sun-dried tomatoes and the goat cheese really
come through. Serve with a rich, full-bodied
California Zinfandel or other fine red wine to fully
appreciate the marriage of flavors.

1	recipe Basic Pizza Dough (page 10) or Sourdough Crust (page 18) olive oil
1	recipe Sun-Dried Tomato Sauce (page 23)
12	ounces goat cheese

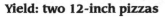

1. Preheat the oven to 450°. Prepare the crust and brush lightly with olive oil.

2. Cover with the sauce and bake for approximately 10 minutes. Remove the pizza from the oven and crumble the cheese over the top. Return to the oven for another 5-10 minutes or until done.

Yield: two 12-inch pizzas

SUMMER GARDEN PIZZA

Everyone with a garden always appreciates another recipe using zucchini. Slices of fresh tomato can be substituted for the tomato sauce. The addition of summer or yellow squash makes for a colorful presentation.

> 1 *recipe Zucchini Crust (page 15)*
> *olive oil*
> 3 *medium zucchinis, thinly sliced*
> 3 *medium summer squash, thinly sliced*
> 1 *teaspoon oregano or marjoram*
> 3 *Tablespoons olive oil*
> 1 *pound mozzarella, grated or sliced*
> 1 *recipe Basic Pizza Sauce (page 21)*

1. Preheat the oven to 450°. Prepare the dough and brush with olive oil.

2. Toss the sliced rounds of zucchini and summer squash with the oregano and sauté lightly in 3 tablespoons oil.

3. Cover the prepared dough with the mozzarella and then spread the sauce over that. Now top with the squash, alternating green and yellow squash in concentric circles around the pizza.

4. Bake for about 20 minutes or until the crust is golden.

Yield: two 12-inch pizzas

Having trouble finding sausage to suit your taste? Simply add the flavors you are missing (garlic, red pepper flakes, fennel, parsley, allspice) when you are cooking the sausage.

Pizza With Sausage & Spinach

This is a wonderful Chicago-style pizza that I never get tired of eating. A good quality sweet Italian sausage, preferably one seasoned with fennel, is my first choice.

1	recipe Chicago-Style Deep-Dish Crust (page 19)
1	pound Italian sausage
1	recipe Basic Pizza Sauce (page 21)
2	pounds fresh spinach
12	ounces mozzarella, grated
$^1/_2$	cup parmesan, grated

1. Preheat the oven to 450°. Prepare the dough and allow to rest.

2. Remove the sausage from the casings, break up coarsely and cook in a skillet over medium heat until no longer pink. Drain excess oil and add to the sauce, bring that to a simmer and cook for about 10-15 minutes.

3. Wash and clean the spinach, chopping coarsely. Heat a skillet and add the spinach, stirring constantly until most of the water has evaporated.

4. Cover the bottom of the pizza with the mozzarella. Combine the spinach and the sauce and fill the pizzas. Top with the parmesan.

5. Bake for about 20-30 minutes or until the crust is golden and the sauce hot and bubbling.

Yield: two 10-inch deep-dish pizzas

Tuna & Red Pepper Pizza with Capers

Here is a pizza made with ingredients most of us have on hand anytime.

  1 recipe Basic Pizza Dough (page 10)
     olive oil
  1 pound mozzarella, grated or sliced
  2 6¹/₂-ounce cans tuna, packed in oil
  1 cup red peppers, roasted and cut in strips
  2 Tablespoons capers
  ¹/₂ cup parmesan, grated

1. Preheat the oven to 450°. Prepare the dough and brush lightly with olive oil.

2. Cover the prepared dough with the mozzarella. Drain the tuna (retain the oil) and crumble over the top. Now cover with the strips of red pepper.

3. Top with the capers and parmesan. Drizzle a tablespoon of the remaining oil from the tuna over the top.

4. Bake for approximately 20 minutes or until the crust is golden and the cheese melted and bubbling.

Yield: two 12-inch pizzas

Always bake a pizza on the floor or lowest rack of your oven. The heat should be concentrated under the pizza to give a crispier crust.

MEATBALL PIZZA

Better than a hero, this meatball pizza is an American classic. Make extra meatballs, keep them in your freezer, and pull them out for spaghetti, pizza, or whatever.

1	*recipe Chicago-Style Deep-Dish Dough (page 19)*
1	*recipe Meatballs (recipe below)*
1	*recipe Basic Pizza Sauce (page 21)*
1	*pound mozzarella, grated*

1. Preheat the oven to 450°. Prepare the dough and let "relax."

2. Add the prepared meatballs to the sauce and let simmer in a medium saucepan for about 20 minutes.

3. Cover the prepared dough with half of the mozzarella, fill the pizzas with the meatballs and sauce, and top with the remaining cheese.

4. Bake for about 20-25 minutes.

Yield: two 10-inch deep-dish pizzas

Meatballs

$1/2$	*pound ground pork or beef*
$1/4$	*cup bread crumbs*
$1/4$	*cup parmesan, grated*
1	*egg, lightly beaten*
1	*clove garlic, finely minced*
2	*Tablespoons parsley, chopped*
	salt and pepper to taste
2	*Tablespoons olive oil*

Combine everything, except the oil, in a mixing bowl. Mix thoroughly. Shape the mixture into approximately 25 small meatballs. In a large skillet, heat the oil, and brown the meatballs, until done, about 10-15 minutes.

Broccoli & Pesto Pizza

This is an original creation that has "quiche-like" qualities. Since broccoli tends to dry out when baked on a thin-crusted pizza, this thicker crust seems to be the perfect answer to combining broccoli and pizza in a non-traditional but delicious dish.

1	recipe Chicago-Style Crust (page 19)
1	large bunch broccoli
$^1/_2$-$^3/_4$	cup Pesto Sauce (page 27)
2	pounds ricotta cheese
12	ounces mozzarella, grated
$^1/_2$	cup parmesan, freshly grated

1. Preheat the oven to 450°. Prepare the dough.

2. Trim the broccoli into florets and skin the stem, chopping it into small pieces. Steam lightly and let drain.

3. In a medium size mixing bowl, cream the pesto and ricotta together. Stir in the broccoli.

4. Line the prepared dough with the mozzarella, fill with the ricotta mixture, and top with parmesan.

5. Bake for approximately 20-30 minutes.

Yield: two 10-inch deep-dish pizzas

GREEK PIZZA

Who would expect pizza to be popular in Greece? But it is, definitely! This original version is a real favorite among some of my friends who won't let me bake anything else when they accept an invitation for dinner at our home.

1   recipe Spinach Crust (page 12)
8   ounces feta cheese
8   ounces ricotta cheese
8   ounces bacon, cut into pieces
1   medium red onion, sliced
1   large, ripe, fresh tomato, sliced
2   Tablespoons olive oil
    freshly ground pepper, to taste

1. Preheat the oven to 375°. Prepare the crust.

2. Let the cheeses come to room temperature while you cook the bacon.

3. Cream the feta and ricotta together and spread evenly over the crust. Crumble the bacon over the top, then cover with the sliced onions and tomatoes.

4. Drizzle the olive oil over the top and bake for about 20 minutes. Top with freshly ground black pepper.

Yield: one 12-inch pizza

Pizza With Zucchini, Sun-Dried Tomatoes & Pine Nuts

This recipe is ideal for hors d'oeuvres, especially if you have mini-tart pans in which to bake the individual servings. If not, use regular tart or quiche pans and, after baking, cut into hors d'oeuvre-size servings.

1	recipe Cream Cheese Crust (page 14)
2	cups zucchini, cut in matchsticks
$^1/_2$	pound mushrooms, sliced
2	Tablespoons garlic, finely chopped
2	Tablespoons shallots, finely chopped
$^1/_2$	cup sun-dried tomatoes in oil, chopped
2	Tablespoons fresh basil, chopped, or 1 teaspoon dried basil
$^1/_4$	cup pine nuts
2·	Tablespoons olive oil
12	ounces mozzarella, grated

1. Preheat the oven to 375°. Prepare the cream cheese crust. Press into tart pans, forming a small edge above the rim of each tart pan. Place these in the refrigerator while preparing the filling.

2. Lightly sauté the zucchini and mushrooms, adding the garlic, shallots, tomatoes, basil, and pine nuts, tossing until everything is coated in oil.

3. Cover the prepared dough with the cheese, spoon the filling over that and bake for about 20-25 minutes.

Yield: two 8- to 9-inch or twelve 3-inch pizzas

Whole Wheat Vegetable Pizza

  1   recipe Whole Wheat Pizza Dough
      (page 12)
  1   pound mozzarella, grated
  1   recipe Vegetable Sauce (page 22)
 $^1/_2$ cup parmesan, grated

1. Preheat the oven to 450°. Prepare the dough.

2. Top the prepared dough with half of the mozzarella. Cover with the sauce and then add the
   remaining cheeses.

3. Bake for about 20-25 minutes or until golden brown.

Yield: two 10-inch deep-dish pizzas

SHRIMP & ARTICHOKE HEART PIZZA

This is an elegant pizza, so bring out the china and silver. I have written the recipe using canned artichokes, not because they're better, but because they're the most readily available. You may want to try frozen or marinated artichokes, or by all means fresh artichokes, if they are in season.

1	recipe Egg Crust (page 17)
2	15-ounce cans artichoke hearts, quartered
1	pound medium shrimp, peeled and deveined
3	Tablespoons olive oil
1	clove garlic, minced
1	pound mozzarella, grated
1	recipe Basic Pizza Sauce (page 21)

1. Preheat the oven to 450°F. Prepare the crust.

2. Combine the artichoke hearts, shrimp, olive oil and garlic in a bowl and toss to coat.

3. Cover the pizza with the mozzarella and then with the sauce. Now arrange the artichokes in concentric circles around the pizza, leaving room for the shrimp to be added later.

4. Bake the pizza for about 10 minutes and remove from the oven. Arrange the shrimp in alternating circles with the artichoke hearts and return to the oven for another 10 minutes or until golden.

Yield: two 12-inch pizzas

Spinach & Bacon Pizza

This pizza ranks among my very favorites. Incredibly simple, it is nonetheless soulfully satisfying.

1	recipe Chicago-Style Deep Dish Crust (page 19)
1	pound bacon
1	recipe Spinach Sauce (page 24)
12	ounces mozzarella, grated
$^1/_2$	cup parmesan or romano, grated

1. Preheat the oven to 450°. Prepare the crust.

2. Chop the bacon strips into quarters and cook until done. Remove with a slotted spoon and stir into the spinach sauce.

3. Line the prepared crusts with the mozzarella, add the sauce and top with the romano or parmesan. Bake for about 20-25 minutes, or until the crust is golden and the filling bubbles.

Yield: two 10-inch deep-dish pizzas

CREOLE PIZZA

Here's evidence of just how American pizza can be. I love New Orleans-style cooking and found myself with some leftover Creole sauce in the refrigerator one day. A few hours later we were eating "Creole Pizza" and it was voted a winner by everyone present.

1   recipe Chicago-Style Deep-Dish Crust (page 19)
1   pound medium shrimp, peeled and deveined
2   Tablespoons olive oil
1   pound mozzarella, grated
1   recipe Creole Sauce (page 25)
2   Tablespoons fresh parsley, chopped

1. Preheat the oven to 475°. Prepare the crust.

2. Toss the shrimp in olive oil and set aside. Cover the prepared dough with the cheese and then the sauce.

3. Bake for about 15 minutes and remove the pizza from the oven. Now arrange the shrimp over the top and return to the oven for another 5-10 minutes, depending on the size of the shrimp. Garnish with the parsley and serve.

Yield: two 10-inch deep-dish style pizzas

CHICKEN ENCHILADA PIZZA

    1   recipe Cornmeal Crust (page 15)
    1   pound cooked chicken meat, diced
  $1/_2$ cup scallions, diced or chopped
    1   teaspoon cumin
    1   cup sour cream
        salt and pepper, to taste
    1   cup Enchilada Sauce (page 26)
    8   ounces monterey jack or cheddar, grated

1. Preheat the oven to 400°F. Prepare the crust in a 10-inch pie pan.

2. While you prebake the crust, mix the chicken, scallions, cumin, sour cream, salt and pepper together.

3. Fill the crust with the chicken mixture, cover with the enchilada sauce, and top with the grated cheese.

4. Bake for approximately 20-25 minutes.

Yield: one 10-inch pizza

Mexican Pizza

Who says pizza has to be Italian? Tacos, burritos, tostadas are all similar to pizzas: they have a "crust," sauce and filling or topping. The ingredients are different, but the results are the same. A satisfying food that's fun to eat and fun to make.

1	recipe Cornmeal Crust (page 15)
1	medium red onion, diced
2	Tablespoons olive oil
3	large tomatoes, peeled, seeded and chopped
4	ounces green chilies, chopped
	salt and pepper, to taste
$^1/_2$	cup chopped scallions
2	Tablespoons cilantro, chopped
2	cups refried beans
8	ounces cheddar cheese, grated
1	ripe avocado
1	cup sour cream

1. Preheat the oven to 400°. Prepare the crust.

2. Lightly sauté the onions in olive oil and then add the tomatoes, green chilies, salt and pepper. Cook until most of the liquid from the tomatoes has evaporated. Add the scallions and 1 tablespoon of the cilantro.

3. Spread the refried beans over the cornmeal crust, add the tomato mixture and top with the cheddar cheese.

4. Bake for about 20 minutes. Slice the avocado and garnish the pizza with the avocado, sour cream and the remaining cilantro.

5. Serve to your lucky guests.

Yield: one 14 x 15-inch or two 8 x 9-inch pizzas

Pizza Rustica

Baked in a pie pan and covered with a crust, this savory pie is similar to a quiche, only better. Rich with an egg and cheese filling, pizza rustica makes a wonderful supper or an impressive brunch dish. It freezes well, so why not make two?

1	recipe Torte Crust (page 16)
4	whole eggs, beaten
1	pound ricotta cheese
$1/_2$	pound sausage, cooked and finely chopped
$1/_4$	pound prosciutto, finely chopped
$1/_4$	pound Canadian bacon, cooked and finely chopped
$1/_4$	cup parmesan, grated
8	ounces mozzarella, grated
$1/_2$	teaspoon oregano or marjoram
2	Tablespoons parsley, chopped
	freshly ground pepper, to taste

1. Prepare the crust, rolling out the dough to cover the bottom of a 9-inch pie pan. Roll out the remainder for the top crust.

2. Preheat the oven to 400°. Combine the eggs and ricotta together, mixing well. Stir in the rest of the ingredients.

3. Fill the crust with this mixture and cover with the remaining dough. Seal the edges and make several slits in the top for steam to escape. Everything can be prepared ahead up to this point, then held in the refrigerator for 3-4 hours, or frozen.

4. With the pie at room temperature, bake at 400° for 15 minutes, then reduce the heat to 325° and bake for another 35-40 minutes, or until the crust is golden.

Yield: one 9-inch pie

Sicilian Pizza

Sicilian pizza is distinguished by its thick, chewy crust and rectangular shape. The dough is allowed to rise three times, twice in the bowl and the third time right on the baking sheet. Any type of sauce or topping will work. Here's one of my favorites.

1	recipe Basic Pizza Dough (page 10)
1	recipe Sauce Putanesca (page 22)
12	ounces mozzarella, grated
$^1/_4$	cup parmesan, grated
$^1/_4$	cup romano, grated

1. Preheat the oven to 400°.

2. Prepare the dough. Once the dough has doubled in bulk, punch it down and allow it to rise again. This time it should only take about 45 minutes.

3. Now punch it down again and roll out the dough to a rectangular shape, slightly larger than a 12 x 17-inch baking sheet. Transfer to baking sheet, building up the edges a little as you work it into shape. Don't despair if you've made a hole somewhere, it can easily be patched up with a bit of excess dough, or simply pinch it together.

4. Now let the dough rise again, approximately 30 minutes. Bake for about 10 minutes.

5. Remove from the oven and dress with the sauce and grated cheeses.

6. Return to the oven. Bake until the edges are golden brown and the cheeses are melted and bubbly, about 10-15 minutes. Cut into squares and serve.

Yield: one 12 x 17-inch pizza

PISSALADIÈRE ▮

No discussion of pizza would be complete without mention of this French cousin of Italian pizza. Originating in the south of France, there are many different recipes, but the constants remain onions, black olives and anchovies. The anchovies are always arranged in a lattice pattern with the olives in the center. You can choose one of many crusts but a pastry crust makes it easy to cut and serve for hors d'oeuvres. Here, then, are two versions of this delicious pizza. Try this recipe using the Cream Cheese Crust (page 14) or Egg Crust (page 17).

1	recipe Basic Pastry Crust (page 10)
$^1/_4$	cup olive oil
3	large yellow onions, finely chopped
2	Tablespoons garlic, minced
1	teaspoon thyme
2	2-ounce tins anchovy filets, rinsed
	about 20 black olives, preferably Niçoise

1. Preheat the oven to 400°. Prepare the crust of your choice into a rectangle slightly larger than a 12 x 17-inch baking sheet. Press up the edges of the dough to form a rim. Place in the refrigerator and let "relax" while preparing the other ingredients.

2. Heat the olive oil in a large skillet and gently sauté the onions over medium heat. Add the garlic and thyme, continuing to stir and cook until the onions are golden in color. This brings out the natural aroma in the onions and gives the dish its distinctive flavor.

3. Remove the dough from the refrigerator and cover with the onion base. Arrange the anchovies across the top in a lattice pattern, then place the olives in the center of each square.

4. Bake for about 20 minutes.

Yield: two 12 x 17-inch pizzas

Pissaladiere II

This version is identical except for the additions of tomato sauce or tomato paste. Follow the instructions for preparing Pissaladiere I through step number 3. Cover the dough with 1 cup Basic Tomato Sauce or 1 6-ounce can tomato paste. Now follow with the onions, anchovies and olives.

Sardines may be substituted for the anchovies, if you prefer. I have also placed tomato slices inside the lattice pattern along with the olives. Capers would be an acceptable substitute for the olives, if necessary.

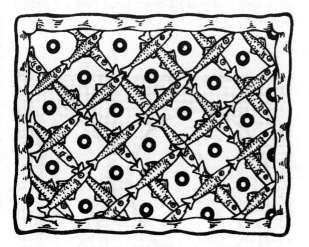

CALZONE

Calzone are members of the pizza family, cousins if you will. Made with pizza dough, they can be filled with a vast array and combination of savory ingredients, then folded over, edges sealed, and baked.

They are just as easy to make as pizza, and for your lucky guests there's the pleasant anticipation of cutting into something that is completely sealed, and inhaling the aromas as they escape from their casing.

Calzone has just begun to surface in some of the most innovative restaurants in the country—funny for a dish that had its beginnings over a hundred years ago.

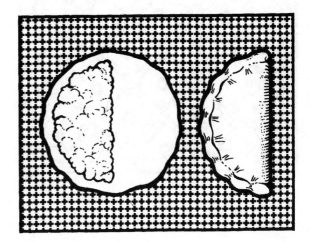

Sausage-Ricotta Calzone

1 recipe Basic Pizza Dough (page 10)
1 pound hot Italian sausage
1 medium onion, diced
1 pound ricotta cheese
8 ounces mozzarella, grated
$1/_4$ cup black olives, pitted and diced
2 Tablespoons olive oil

1. Preheat the oven to 450°. Remove the sausages from their casings, crumble and brown in a skillet over medium heat, adding the onion after the sausage has started to release some fat. Cook until the meat is thoroughly done.

2. Using a slotted spoon, remove the sausage and onion to a large bowl. Blend thoroughly with the ricotta, mozzarella and olives.

3. Roll the dough out into six equal rounds, about 8 inches each. Spoon approximately $2/_3$ cup of filling on one half of each round. Fold over the dough and crimp the edges with your fingers or a fork. (If there is any filling left, you can spread it on French bread and toast in the oven for a delicious snack.)

4. Brush the calzone lightly with olive oil and bake for 20-30 minutes. If you like, the calzone can be assembled several hours in advance and held in the refrigerator, covered with plastic wrap. Calzone also freeze wonderfully, just bake them for about 15 minutes, cool, wrap in foil and freeze. Defrost and reheat.

Yield: six medium calzone

Ham & Cheese Calzone

1	recipe Basic Pizza Dough (page 10)
2	Tablespoons dijon style mustard
2	whole eggs, beaten until frothy
$^1/_2$	pound cooked ham, diced
1	pound gruyere cheese, grated
$^1/_4$	cup parmesan, grated
	freshly ground pepper, to taste
2	Tablespoons olive oil

1. Preheat the oven to 450°. Prepare the dough according to the directions for calzone on page 61. Roll out the dough into six equal rounds, about 8 inches each.

2. Beat the mustard with the eggs, then add the ham, grated cheeses and pepper. Spoon approximately $^2/_3$ cup of filling on one half of each round. Fold over the dough and crimp the edges with your fingers or a fork. Brush with olive oil, and bake the calzone for about 20-30 minutes, or until the crusts are golden.

Yield: six medium calzone

Calzone With Goat Cheese & Prosciutto

1	recipe Basic Pizza Dough (page 10)
4	ounces prosciutto, thinly sliced
8	ounces goat cheese, crumbled
8	ounces Italian fontina or asiago cheese, grated
4	ounces mozzarella, grated
$^1/_2$	teaspoon thyme
1	clove garlic, minced
1	tomato, peeled, seeded and chopped
	freshly ground pepper, to taste
2	Tablespoons olive oil

1. Preheat the oven to 450°. Prepare the dough.

2. Slice the prosciutto into thin strips and combine the cheeses, thyme and garlic in a large bowl, mixing well.

3. Spoon equal amounts of filling onto each of six rounds of dough. Top with the chopped tomato and a dash of pepper.

4. Fold, seal, and brush with olive oil. Bake for about 20-30 minutes or until done.

Yield: six medium calzone

PANZEROTTI

Similar to calzone, but much smaller, panzerotti are often eaten as hors d'oeuvres. Usually they are deep fried rather than baked. Try them either way, both are delicious. Generally the fillings are simpler because the panzerotti are smaller, but experiment with anything that you would put in a calzone, or on a pizza for that matter.

> 1   recipe Basic Pastry Crust (page 13)
> 1   recipe Mornay Sauce (page 24)
> $1/_2$ pound cooked ham, diced
> $1/_2$ cup gruyere cheese, grated
>   pinch cayenne

1. Prepare the dough, roll out about $1/_8$-inch thick, and cut into 3-inch circles using a glass, cup, or cookie cutter.

2. Mix the sauce, diced ham, cheese, and cayenne together and spoon about 1 tablespoon of the filling on half of each round, as for calzone.

3. Fold over and press to seal. If baking, brush with oil, and bake in a preheated 400° oven for 15-20 minutes or until golden brown. If deep-frying, heat the oil to 350° and cook for about 5 minutes, or until done.

Yield: about 15-18 panzerotti

Variations: Sausage-Ricotta filling makes an excellent panzerotti, as does anything with pesto. Yeast doughs can be used as well, though I find the pastry doughs easier to handle for these small finger foods. Try the Cream Cheese Crust (page 14).

INSTANT PIZZA

What to do when you want pizza NOW, and there just isn't time to knead the dough, let it rise, and so on? "Necessity is the mother of invention," and the necessity to have a pizza now has been the starting point for many a successful creation in our home. Here, then is some advice on how best to be prepared for those cravings that can strike at any hour:

CRUSTS

Extra dough in the freezer, rolled out and ready to go is my first choice. In place of this, I have used pita bread, tortillas, English muffins or even good crusty bread.

On my way home I sometimes pick up oven-ready dough from a local pizzeria for a mere $2.00, then I empty the contents of my refrigerator on it for instant gratification. If you're not in such a hurry, I suggest you try one of the several brands of rapid-rising yeasts which are quite acceptable and do save time.

Pizza crust is also available in the dairy case or frozen food section of your grocery, although these prepared crusts yield less than perfect pizza. Foccacia or Boboli style breads can also be used as the base for an instant pizza—you'll find these in the bread aisle or bakery section of your food store.

SAUCES

Sauce presents much less of a problem than crusts. I always have extra cans of whole tomatoes in the pantry. After draining off the liquid, I simply crush the tomatoes over the "dough." Surplus sauces, including pesto, that I have made ahead and frozen, enhance any and all toppings, but in a pinch I admit to having tried several different brands of bottled pizza sauces and they weren't too bad, really.

TOPPINGS

Keep an extra supply of instant pizza fixings around the kitchen: anchovies, sardines, tuna, clams or mussels, artichoke hearts, roasted peppers, olives, capers, dried sausages, and of course—a variety of cheeses. These are the staples for pizza lovers. Some of my best creations are made from combinations of such leftovers as chicken, ham, turkey, onions, zucchini, garlic, fresh tomatoes and other fresh produce.

I try to keep an open mind about potential pizza ingredients beccause half the fun is in the experimenting...so go for it!